ESCAPE FROM SATAN'S ZOO

Acknowledgements

"Escape from Satan's Zoo" is a sequel to the Facebook collaboration, "Satan's Zoo" (2018) by Paul E Anderson, Mike New, Sybil Paradiso, Judith Kirkwood, Colette Marsden, Helen Ramos Markey, Sarah Lyons and Tony Furdock. The poems were written between spring and early summer 2019. Several of the contributors are active animal rescuers. This poem is a tribute to them and to the endangered natural world.

The bestiary contains photographs by Judith Kirkwood, Sarah Lyons, Colette Marsden and one ostensible photo by the editor, Paul E Anderson. The front cover is the painting **Dust Devil** by Sybil Paradiso.The back cover is the painting **Blood Moon Passion** by Colette Marsden.

Special thanks goes to Mike New for his multiple poems and support for the group. We hope you have as much fun reading the book as we had making it.

COOL, CLOUDS AND RAIN

Mike New

Absent the accustomed light,

the heat, the drying out,

lizards lie paralyzed

dead snakes litter the roads

while zombies

with bloodstained eyes

backpacks, walking sticks, and pit bulls

leashed with a clothesline rope,

wander the hills

like those in houses

with their burden of neuroses

consuming their own fancies

trying to discover the relationship

between the phenomenon of being

and the being of phenomenon.

Paul E Anderson I read it at a snail's pace. Absent the accustomed light [STOP] the heat, the drying out, [STOP], etc.

Paul E Anderson OK. I want to make the second edition of "Satan's Zoo" but need a title. "Satan's Zoo Revisited"? "Re-Zoo"? Help me, Sybil and any of the other authors, please.

Christy Anderson **ESCAPE**

A LIST OF THINGS THAT ARE _____

A woman in a _____ rain
A _____ road, a _____ haircut
_____ manners, _____ ice
on a sidewalk
Mr./ Ms. _____, the poet
_____ hair
diving into the _____ pool
_____ skin
_____ drums, _____ vibes
_____ dialogue
_____ spots, _____ lines
all _____ as _____.

Paul E Anderson Colette did a wonderful poem last time with the word "luminous"? Maybe Sybil could try it again. Helen? You just think of a word.

Paul E Anderson I think I'm going to submit this to the UIndy literary magazine. It would be a blast doing the reading (there's a READING!) by handing out pencils and the fill-in-the-blank form and then reading the resultant poems to the audience (authors). I would have to limit the number read aloud at the reading but everyone would get to keep their poem. Or someone else's poem. They could trade poems! The poem gets better and better in my mind.

Paul E Anderson Oh, remember, you can either copy and paste the original (blanks) and replace the blanks with your word, or, just comment the word and I will put it into the poem.
Paul E Anderson Maybe it's not as good as I thought.
Paul E Anderson I'm depressed.

A LIST OF THINGS THAT ARE BAD
A woman in a bad rain
A bad road, a bad haircut
bad manners, bad ice
on a sidewalk
Ms. Bad, the poet
Bad hair
diving into the bad pool
bad skin
bad drums, bad vibes
bad dialogue
bad spots, bad lines
all bad as bad

Red Headed Agama - Judith Kirkwood

A LIST OF THINGS THAT ARE _____

I'm putting this poem/game back up because I like it so much. Bless its blank little heart. I made a couple minor edits.

A LIST OF THINGS THAT ARE _____

A man/woman in a _____ rain
A _____ road, a _____ haircut
_____ manners, _____ ice
on a sidewalk
Ms./Mr. _____, the poet
_____ hair
diving into the _____ pool
_____ skin
_____ drums, _____ vibes
_____ dialogue
_____ spots, _____ lines
all _____ as _____.

Mike New **A List of Things that are Needed**

A woman in a boring rain
A deserted road, a new haircut
odd manners, black ice
on a sidewalk
Mr. Knowit, the poet
long hair
diving into the office pool

smooth skin

steady drums, jumping vibes

whispered dialogue

special spots, licked lines

all given as received.

Sybil Paradiso Mike New I like it that you didn't follow the rules on this one. The parts I liked best, though, were, "Mr. Knowit, the poet-

Steadily drums, jumping vibes

whispering dialogues."

Mike New There are rules?

Colette Marsden **A List Of Things That Are Gentle**

A woman in a gentle rain

A gentle road, a gentle haircut

Gentle manners, gentle ice on a sidewalk

Ms/Mr Gentle, the poet

Gentle hair

Diving into a gentle pool

Gentle skin

Gentle drums, gentle vibes

Gentle dialogue

Gentle spots, gentle lines

All gentle as gentle

Sybil Paradiso **A woman in a nasty rain**

A nasty road, a nasty haircut

Nasty manners, nasty ice on a sidewalk

Ms. Nasty, the poet

Nasty hair

Diving into a nasty pool
Nasty skin
Nasty drums, nasty vibes
Nasty dialogue
Nasty spots, nasty lines
Nasty, nasty, nasty.

Tony Furdock I'll get back to you when I can spend some time with this.

Black-throated Green Warbler - Sarah Lyons

A DEATHBED CONFESSION

Mike New

"I am about to die, but God will surely take care of you, and you shall carry my bones up from here." Genesis 50:25

"You have to believe,"

she said one afternoon

"that some meaning

is attached to every word."

There's a bus honking

an avenue away.

"You have to trust

that some people will

help if they possibly can."

As she said that she rubbed her hands

red now on the knuckles, and I wondered.

Not the words

but the wonder lies only in misapprehension

even ignorance.

How can Hell's children

ever believe they might even

echo more than

a snatch of a song

mathematical riddles

what the crow

given enough time

will finally figure out,

repeat, translate

even if Gabriel

intermediates,

something of what might

make us eternal?

From Port Chicago

to the mothballed fleet

the wind sings

through the electrical wires

on the broad thin shoulders

of giant steel skeletons

trudging down the side of the hill

deer everywhere

the marsh hawk

hovering and crying

to its mate in the eucalyptus trees

in the valley

where the train,

on the tracks

that skirt the water

carries tar sands

toward San Pablo Bay.

THE STIRRINGS

Mike New

The fog horn sounds like a huge cow

searching for her calf

or the rest of the herd

in the middle of the straits.

Near town as we ascend a steep hill

the roar of the warplanes below the clouds

obliterates everything else

on our walk in the mist.

Anxious for the fawns

we've begun to see,

we search assiduously

as our reputation demands

for broken glass to pick up.

Rain falls irregularly

at various tempos

but in the same steady

unsyncopated rhythm.

Wild cucumber vines,

their skin covered by

minute filaments

that in larger plants

develop into burrs or briars,

strike out on the ground

and up the still leafless bushes

like thin green snakes.

A lizard finds a crack in a bay laurel nut

and eats into it desperately or greedily

until his scaly head gets stuck inside.

I stoop in sudden welcome sun

and carefully removed the tiny shell.

The lizard pauses a moment

to regain his bearings

then waddles quickly

over the cucumber vines.

On the uphill edge of the road

a cubical rock the color of rust

and the size of a small washing machine

slips down the muddy hill

onto the side of the road

flanked by to hummocks of green grass

that I imagine the deer nibbling

in the middle of a rainy night

when they leave the prints of their feet

in the mud at the side of the road

so that we'll know how they are doing.

CLIMATE CHANGE

Paul E Anderson

The shadows gradually disappear
as the sun rises

like the penumbral effect
in Roe vs. Wade

We are all shadows
disappearing

as the clouds vanish
and the species expires

A cat just crossed your shadow
as you sat dreaming

about women's liberation
Let's hope we have that chance

LIKE A PRAYER

Colette Marsden

Prose poems. I could write prose poems. That would solve the line ending problem. I must thank Maxine as usual for reminding me about prose poems. Saying and not saying, like a bell unrung. I can fix that later. It's a prose poem; it doesn't have to rhyme or anything. I'll think of a better simile for "saying without saying." Like something else. Or better yet, I could make it into a Fill-in-the-Blank poem and let the reader (listener) fill in the appropriate simile. Like

_____.

Show 14 Replies

Sybil Paradiso Sorry, you said one word. Like maybe wormwood.

Paul E Anderson Both work. Thanks, Sybil.

Colette Marsden Like the sound of silence

Colette Marsden Like pantomime

Colette Marsden Like Osmosis

Colette Marsden Like a still leaf

Colette Marsden Like a prayer

BASEMENT MOVES

Sybil Paradiso

She was chased down the stairs

By the old iron rake

Dirty metal spikes looming and bouncing over her hair

Threatening to comb the back of her head.

She escaped into the dark flooded basement

Barefooted, she splashed and dashed

Making it to the old coal room and slamming the door

Escaping the rake but now

Surrounded by spirits of turpentine

And shelves with mason jars containing the remaining products

Of last years harvest-

tomatoes, peaches, pickled cucumbers.

Next level, specimens in formaldehyde.

A carcinomic liver, a spider monkeys' heart and a 2-headed fetus.

Gradually, she came to realize that she had been sleepwalking.

She was standing in the old coal room

door shut

In front of a shelf bearing last year's garden preserves

And a can of Spirits of

Turpentine.

Awake now, she makes her way to the door but hesitates

Listening, before cautiously opening.

Alligator - Judith Kirkwood

BEING MEANING FOR A FAWN

Mike New

Do furred and thick-skinned
deer or cow,
constantly nipping
and chewing
the warm fluorescent green grass
emerging at that moment
from the close comfort of the Earth,
speculate,
swishing or flipping
the tiny elongated ball of white fluff
or the long thick shit covered whip
of a bull,
on the value or meaning
of what they're doing?

While the four older others discreetly
not wanting to eat in front of others
move slowly into the coyote bushes
the one no more than
two weeks older than a fawn
legs more comfortable standing still
than moving off like the others
eyes like large buckeye seeds
speculating
tail swinging gladly
from side to side
staring at
the two-legged creatures
hiking the same hard road again
in the rain,
traveling first one way
then a short time later
the other,
stopping only

to pick up
things that smell bad
and are often hard on the hooves.

LIVING ALONE IN SOUTH FLORIDA

Judith Kirkwood

Every room

has a whirligig ceiling fan

to stir the air.

All day and all night

I hear the gentle clack and clatter

of vertical blinds swaying

like storks whispering secrets.

On a good day

I am awash in puffy bursts

of spun gusts,

able to levitate

above alligators gliding

soundlessly

through the swamp

of memory,

barely rippling

reflections of clouds.

Bee - Judith Kirkwood

AMBIENT SOUNDS

Sybil Paradiso

When our landlady built her villa on this corner of the mountainside, the dog was already there. He obligingly allowed her to build a house, and now he stands at the corner of Ladrillera y Arboles and proudly barks out his territory all night long.

Not only has his property been vastly improved, but he now also has a job. He is king of his own little hill in San Miguel. But there are many little hills here and many mongrels proclaiming themselves king. People get a sense of security when they hear lots of dogs barking throughout the night. They sleep peacefully, knowing their dogs are awake and watchful. If the dogs were to stop barking, the people would feel as alerted as though the many church bells had ceased ringing.

The boundaries of each dog's territory are explicitly marked off, several times throughout the night. He runs around the perimeter of his estate barking to near and distant neighbors, occasionally stopping to lay his scent. At approximately 7:00 A.M. the dogs begin to quiet down, leaving the auditory field open for the lazy cocks, who never wake at dawn. They are followed quickly by the workers early morning rock breaking ceremony.

This signals the dogs to drop off into slumber throughout the neighborhood with a sense of peace and security knowing their territory is being worked on and improved by men. These are not domesticated animals; they are mangy unkempt proprietors of the land. They have no desire to be petted; they walk away from humans' baby dog talk. They are not mean animals, although when they are standing above you on a ledge barking, they seem quite ferocious. A few scraps of food towards rent is all they require; you may come and go as you please.

CROWNED WITH WILDFLOWERS

Mike New

Armed with good intentions and grand hopes

they hop off their accustomed trail and hike

up into the high hills where the wildflowers flourish

away from the sun stealing shade of the trees

in the dark valleys below.

At once within the heavy headed grasses

both native and foreign vetch intrude

from the edges of the path

its purple and violent petals pendants

fluttering just slightly in the wind

in ranks and rows like ancient Chinese armies

poised to charge the invading Jurkins.

The week before, the soap root plants

were big with blooms

but something, apparently, the deer

have eaten all the flowers.

The yarrow flowers are like tiny white clouds

floating across a green sky at our feet.

Out of the amphitheater high up on the side of an outcropping,

California poppies arrayed in orange robes wave

to the actors—the Ass and the Queen of the Fairies—

bantering about love in the comedy below.

TRYING TO SLEEP

Paul E Anderson

to Ursula K. Le Guin

Intrusive thoughts

Cesar Vallejo

The fractured spirit

The bang

of the gavel

The dreams of the dispossessed

The whistle

of a cardinal

Childhood memories

A first kiss

Death's approach

Breathing

This endless thought

Map of stars

ENDURING SPRING

Mike New

The Canada geese have returned again
despite the fact that apparently
what we have to offer
doesn't altogether please them.
They stand on the rotted piers
at the edge of the still muddy water
escaping to the ocean through the straits
honking bitterly in their dissatisfaction.

The trajectory of two is never quite the same
no one's to blame because what contains
so much meaning will inevitably trip on the truth
like a child growing tired of jumping
trips on the rope with anger and disappointment.

The tiresome days of leprous old age
endlessly unroll in a monotonous
repetition of excuses
that no longer even matter
with what half of the heart has survived
the ordeal of merely surviving
now hidden in frustration's rage

KEY

Paul E Anderson

I sit on the patio
and listen to the birds
Today, they are a musical score
A staff, time signature, and key
written on the wind
(a 1956 Technicolor melodrama film
Except for the lyricism
no reason to care
Flights
down a winding stair
Flights
morning to night
strings strummed
on the blue guitar
robins, swallows, wrens
sounds
A minor pleasure
with no other measure

MARCH WIND

Mike New

Along the river and the railroad tracks

the wind off the ocean roars

emerging in the rejoicing of reaching land

to run through the trees

and past the houses

past squirrels and scrub jays

galloping like wild stallions

up into the foothills to the mountains

where lighter now and diminishing

the wind and the wild horses

dance in the snow

like tornados of knives

Judith Kirkwood Does this keep the same spirit, or diminish your message:

March Wind

Along the river and the railroad tracks

The wind off the ocean rejoices

As it hits land,

Roughing up the trees,

Scudding past the houses,

Past squirrels and scrub jays,

Scattering their nuts and seeds,

Rumbling and thumping

Like wild stallions

As it heads into the foothills,

Is blocked by the mountains,

And, diminishing,

Dances in the snow,

But slaps our faces

With needles of cold.

The night will bring

Tornados of knives.

Smiley Face Mussels - Colette Marsden

IDENTIFYING BIRD SONGS

Paul E. Anderson

Sometimes I sit on the patio and watch the sun rise

The neural net of the naked trees

just entering Spring

Tuesday, March 12, 2019

The sky through the branches

pink and blue in alternate bands

a future flag

A bird I cannot name

flies to a branch and whistles

"Too, too, too

tapping

on a true jingle

https://en.wikipedia.org/wiki/Bird_vocalization

ANIMAL SOULS

Judith Kirkwood

Children are born with an animal spirit, a nahual that follows them like a shadow. - Randy Malamud (quoting Rigoberta Menchu), **Poetic Animals and Animal Souls**, 2003, P. 57.

My first husband

had the eyes of a hawk.

He saw the falling star

while I searched the darkness

and saw nothing.

His gaze was riveting,

pinning you in place,

as if you were chloroformed

so you didn't flutter

while under observation.

Dad's got the crazy eyes

our younger son would say,

the luminescence

of the blue gray or gray green

orbs uncanny

under a silky black unibrow.

He was a magician

without a wand,

a shapeshifter

when it came to distinguishing

the forest from the trees.

My second husband's nahual
was undoubtedly a bear.
He was furry,
scary when angry,
and hibernated almost constantly.
When facing a grizzly
your best bet is to play dead.
But if encountering a black bear
you must stand and fight.
I could never figure out
which kind of bear he was,
so I mostly ran away
if I saw a clear path.
That's just my perception though.
He sees himself as a wild boar
charging things just to knock them over,
swinelike in his approach to life.
My spirit animal may be a monkey,
swinging from limb to limb,
endlessly grooming, nitpicking,
social, happy, protective
of our young.
Old World monkeys
can be found at temples.
New World monkeys
try to avoid being used
in lab experiments.

In my next life,
I would like to be guided
by a mockingbird,
singing through the night
during mating season,
performing concerts on a wire,
speaking many languages.

DURING A WARM RAIN

Mike New

In the house, all the faucets drip

a steady persistent dirge

like the regular sad fall

of the hooves of horses

pulling a flag-draped coffin.

During the Jurassic Period

water stood on fifty percent

more of the Earth's surface

than it does today.

We have not only been

for twelve or fifteen

thousand years

relatively cool

we have also been

relatively dry.

The best scientific evidence

indicates that our dry cool days

are rapidly coming to an end

to the delight of mosquitoes,

algae, fungi, and mold.

RECEIPT

Paul E Anderson

Carolyn was working at the grocery store so, naturally, I stood in her checkout lane.

There was a woman in front of me who was gabbing with Carolyn.

I said to the woman, "So, you're one of Carolyn's buddies too?".

She answered in a voice so shy, it was almost inaudible. "Yes."

Carolyn thought it was a hoot, two of her grocery store friends talking to each other.

When it was my turn, I told Carolyn about my wife's condition.

She sent her best wishes. We talk about gardening and her fishing trips to Florida.

She remembered that my wife had not been to the store recently.

She waved off reading the amount of my fuel points, handing the receipt to me, "You can read this."

Ducks (New Zealand Papango) - Sarah Lyons

SONG

Paul E Anderson

A half sonnet
should fit on a gro-
cery list, drawn on
the back of a gro-
cery receipt. Get
tuna fish, eggs, ba-
king soda, psyllium
(sp?
The reverse side is
intention. The printed
side realization. Too
much? Yes, but

only the cost, not
the song itself

BLOOD

Sybil Paradiso

Yesterday Nichole and I were walking past the farmacia on Reloj.
Nichole darted inside the shop and asked the man, who spoke good
English, if he had any Bloody Potatoes. I tried to stop her but couldn't
get to her in time. He looked puzzled and answered, none that he
knew of. When she explained to him that she had meant the
marzipan candies, he nodded and pointed to the shelf where they
were kept and said they seemed to be out of what we thought were
Bloody Potatoes and went on to explain that what we had assumed to
be potatoes were actually something called mamays, a fruit that
resembles a potato on the outside and is red inside. He also assured
us that the lady would be making more. Still, that doesn't explain the
scabby peaches or blood streaked bananas.

At the bullfight, B.J. got a bloody bull's ear. The matadors threw it into
the stands; it whizzed past our heads to the hands of a guy sitting
behind us, who tossed it back to B.J. It was caked with blood and
dust & the bright white cartilage gleamed in the sun. It's not like a
baseball game where everybody wants to keep the ball. As we left
the arena, there was the blood of dead bulls everywhere we walked.
They dragged the last dead bull past us, through the bloody street.
My shoes kept sticking to the cobblestone. People stroked the bulls'
horns, I guess for luck, or etched the sign of the cross on its
forehead. B.J. carried his bull's ear away in a cup, When it first
dropped, it appeared to still be moving. We all handled it with care.

Black Vultures - Sarah Lyons

FEAR

Mike New

My enemy's rage escapes
through a large mouth
loudly loaded with puffs

of smoke and flashes

like lightning in a mirror,

and, equally as insidious

to our common hope,

prepares to devour me at night

in the middle of a dream.

 To catch metaphors,

like butterflies,

to illustrate the entire tale

of how much wickedness

has been spied

everywhere without pause

would consume what light

remains in the Universe.

My enemy has become a vampire

a bloodless gray face

torn by a violent expression

the painful glare from savage eyes

matted hair, nappy bearded,

dirty, slipshod without socks

sweeping dirt into smoke like dust.

SUNDAY EVENING

Paul E Anderson

The church bells cease ringing
and there is a silence like listening

for the next sound
trepidation, expectation

I hear my wife's breath next to me
a rodeo

She is dreaming about sailing into a harbor
and setting up the bronc-busting

on Wall Street
and that end of Manhattan Island

The church bells cease ringing
and there is a silence like listening

GLORY TO WHAT'S NOT IN A NAME

Mike New

The daffodil is not

the feathery orange areola

in the center of the circle

of translucent yellow petals

like tongues lapping up the sunshine.

The thing is not the name.

Our minds create the thing

from our perceptions,

so things exist only in our minds,

and when we try to share

the things within us

with someone else,

we have nothing to help us but names.

THIS IS _____

Paul E Anderson As an example of what we did in the first book, Satan's Zoo, here is the very first fill-in-the blank poem:

THIS IS _____

This is _____.
These are living _____.
Now _____ and _____.
We're _____.

THIS IS AN EXAMPLE
This is a bee.
These are living beings.
Now the bees are dying and so are we.
We're animals.

Sybil wrote about a lizard under her house.

Helen Ramos Markey Got one already I just wrote it. Coincidence it's called **This**. How funny. I've been having psychic phenomena all week. Full moons do that to me.

Tony Furdock

The "Shelter"

This is difficult

These are living creatures

Now they're staring at a blank concrete wall

And wondering what happened

We're a sick society

THIS

Helen Ramos Markey

To my dog

I am thinking, if I could
I could pinch my fingers just so
As if to indicate the possible
Thread of a thought
Or a scrap
Of a scone, or a bread
And toss that "off the cuff"
And you,
With your whiny eyes,
Chin,
Dripping a bead
Of saliva
Just so
Does that signify, then, every morsel or scrap
Or ditched last half of a spoon or carafe
Or a dip, and some lettuce
Tuna,
Salad
Or baked, grilled cheese
Should be yours too if you please?
Can
You stop
That bead
Of saliva
And Sit........
Sit......
And here's the rub,
You will wait,
For Godot, Jesus Christ, the Year of Reckoning,
Prince's prediction,
And still, didn't you know?
They came, and went,
That, and some snow
In June, packages, mail, men came and went,

Doorbells and hands
Muzzle ready
Ruffled you
Then steady went away,
And still you sit…
Sit.…
And patiently stay
In your fitful way.
With eyes
That defy
The mystery of you,
Your universe,
Your scent,
And how you can find,
Anything, anywhere, if it is mine,
With those eyes that whine.
Those amazingly shiny,
Clear, opalesque, obtrusive eyes
In your fur-encased soul
Cargo, catapulting
The streets on our daily trot,
Clitter clatter your nails,
Turn
Sniff, talk to the air,
Lift a leg, drop a scent,
Traverse the back stairs
On the cusp of twilight,
And you, seem to have a hand
(or a paw) at helping the sun to slowly fade, because night
That is your time,
You,
A bundle of wondrous, speculative joy
Who tremble upon my return everyday,
And muzzle your hand,
Into my balled-up fist,
To remind me, retell me
Through centuries, remember,
This
Is your kiss.

IN PRAISE OF MICE AND BIRDS

Mike New

A mouse
except when she eats
through the walls
is a quiet animal
speaking in a squeaky
little voice
hard to hear
unless the old woman lies down
on the floor
in her nightgown
and listens carefully
for much of the night,
her arms pulled close
to her sides,
her toes curled up,
growing cold
then being cold
then enjoying being cold,
feeling numb
drugged
then crawling
back into bed
to sleep until
the sun comes
over the hills
and warms her.

The sun
raises the bird
from the death
of her sleep,

and she's a noisy,
curious, determined
creature who flits
and hops from what
might be good to eat
over here
to what looks
appetizing
over there,
gormandizing
on the crumbs
left by the dog
under the picnic table
on the leeward side
of the dunes
so the sound
of the bird's exultation
flies in the open window
on the rays of the warming sun
as the old woman sits
still in her nightgown
her hands,
one holding a spoon,
beside a white plate
and on the plate
several raw cashews
a date
and various
multicolored pills
for Parkinson disease.

JUST SPRING

Paul E Anderson

It's just-Spring
and the birds are chirping

Not a metaphor
for a country collapsing

Sounds
and color

in a poem
Words

finding a nest
winging

from one breast
to another

LIVING IN MIDAIR

Mike New

The deer path through the hills
that we follow on Sundays
to avoid all the cars
on their way to bars
to watch games on TV
to forget and to have fun
as if the base of their beliefs
the root of their tree produced
what amuses without strengthening.

A sad, sour, old bird with a beard
a turkey-cock displaying up the hill
claims that fear initiates knowing:
fear first that you don't know much
then fear that new knowledge
will rattle your home off its foundation
and recreating the world
you surmise yourself will be tiring,
difficult, and disheartening.

Having been born has not brought sufficient
warrant to the ceaseless rebirth
reawakening to the world
with wonderful surprise

day after day,

when we would rather

slumber in recasting the past

or imaging what the future

might possibly be

chiefly all to no good

economic end

reckoning the spirit of the age

instant karma becoming bitcoins.

Instead of discovery, decision, conflict

and change, being the protagonist

in our own happy ending,

we fill our time with distractions

from what is more dissatisfying

than most want to admit.

Yet, though, fear, the prophet said,

the first step off the edge of the cliff.

we need to learn to live while falling.

Maybe, if we work together,

we'll invent wings for ourselves

on our way to the dirt.

LEARNING BIRD SONGS (NUTHATCH)

Paul E Anderson

I go out on the patio

and listen to the birds again

A red-breasted nuthatch, female

calls in the morning

back and forth

Another bird answers twittering

probably the male

The female

answers as Mae West

"Pretty, pretty, pretty

Grackle - Sarah Lyons

LUNCH WITH ECKHART TOLLE

Mike New

Every day, I ask myself and others
like you why so many people

are so unhappy?

I'll admit that I don't know the answer

but I know that the two most powerful emotions

that all we share are envy and ambition.

"I want," squawks the gray seagull

soaring over the white belly

of the dead black bass

floating fast in the river's swift current

and the powerful outflowing tide.

To create palaces out of the imagination

we are forced to fancy meanings

about the world and everything in it.

We call them words but more often

they are metaphors allowing us in dirt

to taste seasoned with a touch of faith

the abiotic become the image of a god.

The happiest human I know is a dog

who, in living in harmony with nature,

has become a most virtuous creature.

We political creatures

live by laws other than nature's.

We want

whereas one's dog simply accepts.

Timon of Athens

or Crates of Thebes

what did the human race

learn from either of these

but that to die poor

and unknown

was a finer testament

to worth

than all the Trump Towers on Earth.

MINUTIAE

Paul E Anderson

Tired in general
Focus on minutiae

Auditory
Images

Moments
Metaphors

creating metaphors
intuition

Bird songs
Birds flying

Calls
trills

Minutiae
Latin, literally 'trifles

Latin, literally 'trifles
Minutiae

trills
Calls

Birds flying
Bird songs

intuition
creating metaphors

Metaphors
Moments

Images
Auditory

Focus on minutiae
Tired in general

A TRIP TO THE SNOW

Mike New

This year the snow is not far away
a short drive on a warm day.

The monotonous white
lying spent now
on the sides of the mountains
demands to be known
by shapes and lines
created in the phase shift
of rain into snow
while being driven
by a desperate wind.

In an old orchard
where deer at night
pass through
and where during the day
men with dogs on leashes
and young women
beside uberous cheeked children
circle the outlines of the trees
projected by the sun
onto the snow.

NOISE

Paul E Anderson

The yard guys are out at 7:00 AM
Sounds like twirled six-guns, bang, bang, bang

Which will continue until noon
when they take lunch

I can't hear the birds
I remember certain parts from yesterday

A duet, a call and response
Three crows flying north

A robin listening quizzically
to a chorus of frogs

MAKING LOVE ON A HILL IN THE SUN

Mike New

In the warm uphill sunlight
impatient like the sparrows

at the crossing of the streets

waiting for her to step away

from all the many others

and to be again for me alone

love tangled up in insight and foresight

like the relentless wise tide tugging

at the weary river broken hearted

already pushed by generations

and dragged by the anonymous ocean.

Hiking to the brick factory, love singing

while the prefrontal cortex remains silent

proclaims to eager ears through

both disappointment and satisfaction

the inadequacy of beauty

and the body's many languages,

the wisdom learned at birth and in dying.

NOTHING BUT BLUE SKIES FROM NOW ON

Paul E Anderson

https://www.popularmechanics.com/science/environment/a26553617/clouds-disappear-study/

When the atmospheric CO2 level rises enough

it will dispel the clouds, according to a recent experimental model.

The striking aspect

is the time frame: less than a hundred years

Some children born today will still be alive. The sky will be clear,

night and day

There's a connection between clouds and rain

A world without clouds will have no rain. Without rain, all life on earth

will perish

not just the bees, but all insects, birds, plants, yes, all human beings,

even microorganisms, except possibly in the sea

Even in the oceans, where refuge may be sought, the water

temperature

under an atmosphere without the filtering grace of clouds will likely kill

all life

THE DEAD SNAKE

Mike New

It is the common thing which is anonymously about us." William Carlos
Williams

All day the hot sun marches
on the road above their homes
and at night with only a weak wind
their sleep is interrupted by sounds
that threaten then suddenly disappear,
so wakes the sleeping snakes and lizards.

This is written on the wall of a cave
where voices of drunken women
can be heard in the empty darkness
where the cave tempts the poet
into Earth's interior
late at night
in the winter
when the force of a god's footfall
forces warm wet air up from the southwest
and the wind smells like whales.

Bits of fluff
torn by the wind
from the cottonwood trees
sail crazily out above our heads
swinging in long descending arcs
that end abruptly
the wind being now blocked by the trees
so the fluff falls slowly
trembling as it drops
like tiny snowflakes.

The red plum
and the rarer yellow
hide tiny fruit
beneath their garnet leaves.

A company of red clover
in tall red hats
stands at attention
below an old rusted
barbed wire fence
still nailed to a blackened
wooden post
now jutting horizontally
out from the side of the hill.

At one point
our paths separate
so she's hidden downhill
behind a live oak tree
when she calls.

In front of a culvert
lies the dead snake
on its back
a young gopher snake
bluish on the sides of its white belly
half cut when the tire
crushed then rolled
the snake rising early
to meet the promise
of the warming day.

ZUCCHINI AND WILD RICE WITH SHRIMP

Paul E Anderson

I cooked zucchini and wild rice

and, while the rice was cooking, washed the

dishes

I believe if men across the globe would do this

women would be a lot happier

I think of it as an issue

It is not about one sex being superior

to the others

You cook the zucchini and the shrimp

The rice must be tender

but not too tender

CANTA, CANTA

Judith Kirkwood

As the mockingbird commences vespers

my sister and I unfold our sling chairs

on the side of the road to listen

in the slanting light.

Sis, a band director,

raises her hands to conduct.

The leaves have already hushed.

We are lucky the repertoire tonight

is birdsongs, and not the mockery

of sirens, frogs, crickets, or me crying.

Many a day have I washed this road with tears,

and I know this particular mocker

can imitate the whir of a washing machine

as well as dive-bomb my head

and fight off a hawk.

My sister is stupefied by the triple tongue trilling,

changes in pitch, and other vocal gymnastics.

I want to believe these hours-long concerts

are more than a breeding mechanism.

I read that a mockingbird can imitate a dusky

seaside sparrow

that has been extinct for 15 years.

I read that the sound echoes

off of houses and down hillsides.

I have observed that they broadcast

from places of eminence,

the tippy-top of a tall pole,

from which they will rocket vertically,

landing with grace and skill,

continuing to sing.

The plumescence of a male peacock's tail feathers

cannot touch this bird's showmanship.

It's time to go, I nudge.

My sister does not yet know

that our friend will also sing

between 10 pm and 3 am,

never exhausting its repertoire.

And that if you walk away

and keep walking for miles

you will enter the territory

of another mockingbird,

blanketing the land

with tales from birddom,

also replicating the jake brake

of an 18-wheeler

and the excitement of four chihuahuas

who bark at their own shadows.

CAMERA

Paul E Anderson

To be the cathedral of reason that grows as in summer when Daphne produces a single twig, leaves silvered. - Maxine Chernoff

A video

of the tulip tree

with fireflies

is foolish

All black

a few

flashes

Beware

I am poison

I am love

Erratically

Evanescent

Damselfly - Sarah Lyons

PREPARING FOR OBLIVION

Mike New

Late at night, the cold wind
blows in from the northwest
producing passing through the apple tree's
limbs already hanging down with small apples
a roaring, almost animalistic, sound
as if the whales dying on the beaches
sang one last song in sinking toward extinction.
During the hot and cloudy day,
my neighbors relentlessly

saw and hammer on their houses
like Noah and his sons,
hearts fill with desperation,
pounding feverishly
on the promise in the ark.
Everybody tells me
I'm going to be caught off guard
if I don't follow
what's going on
by watching TV.
I feel what's happening though
as the rain again begins to fall
and hear it in the frantic churring sparrows
under the tiles on the roof over my head,
a roof that leaks when it rains.

WINE

Paul E Anderson

A biplane drags a sign advertising Stella Rosa wine
It's Memorial Day weekend

and a lot of people must buy wine
You can buy wine on Sunday now

in Indiana
The sky is clear

the birds are drunk
The hour is early afternoon

Clouds, then rain
Be careful, driving

Great Blue Herons - Judith Kirkwood

THE EARLY RISING SNAKE

Mike New

truth
he only just in early winter
dragged himself
to that insufficient bed

avoiding the mud once again

slowed by boredom and fat with luck

the oldest of the snakes
that lie along the path
on the margin of the creek
between the hemlock
and the bay laurel tree

resignedly, regally, he abides
the cold wind and the vicious rain
like rocks rolled down the hill
onto the thorny leaves
under which he lay

so slightly covered

the old snake first feels the sun
and the aching in his empty belly

he lifts his little olive head
and tastes
with a tiny red bifurcated tongue
the sun and the flavor of the air

having learned through
his uncoiled nucleosomes
that survival of lying drunk
on a bench in a cold rain

demands the same passion
for the pleasures of the body
and of the soul
that brought him to a bed
instead of to his grave
 slowly he slips out
onto the warm clay

Fish with Eyebrows - Sarah Lyons

PROPERTIES OF GLASS

Paul E Anderson

The glass is warped
in the northwest room
where I have so often watched the sun
Glass melts
over time and the images are distorted
The windows face Atlantic Street
cutouts in a disoriented fantasy
A woman's head bobs along like a dolphin
a white-haired woman talking
on a cell phone
The straight lines
and the warped lines interact
to draw a theoretical beach
next to a crazy sea
Ripples in sand.
An old man climbing the hill
on Brill

THE BUTTERFLY CAMPAIGN

Mike New

Periodically, a species of butterfly
called popularly "painted ladies"
marauds through the area
in a butterfly manner.

Announced by an occasional appearance
by what can be mistaken at first as the shadow
of a bird or a muddy leaf blown off the trunk
of the nearby overhanging coastal live oak tree
or it might be mistaken for a moth
as it enters a shaft of light sliding down the hill
between the trees
except that a moth at this time of year
would be more unusual than a butterfly.

The tide of awkwardly flapping butterflies
swells rapidly,
driven by a strong wind from the south
they
like confused cats
each acts independently
and with no apparent destination
except not back into the powerful wind.

Eventually, their bodies,
some with still flickering wings,
strew the ground, the bushes, and the trees
like the bodies of dead soldiers at Waterloo.

HOW I PREPARE TO WRITE

Paul E Anderson

I stop doing what I was doing. I look out the window
The branch of a tree
birds, clouds, reverie
Words

CRY BABY

Mike New

If I'm crying when you see me

you'll forgive me and not worry

because crying's a personal thing

not a hotel for squatters

who understand your contradictions

coolly calculating

what when you cry

you understand

like a fire blown by the wind

burning through the tall dry grass.

Cry for the burnt grass

the bugs and birds and lizards

but too for the leaping

flames and smoke like incense

rising into the sapphire sky.

Even a quiet passion

the tear on the cheek

the sigh

thins the chill

that has settled on the bones.

Crying's an intrapersonal communication

a gesture from the mind to the heart

the word become water

our warm mother.

MEMORIAL DAY 2019

Paul E Anderson

Today the tulip tree

is all the sailors lost at sea.

Wave and sway

and sail to a better day.

from a war not heaven sent.

Today this is their monument.

GOING HOME TO INDIANA

Mike New

The window at the foot of my boyhood bed
faced down toward the junction
of the Ohio River and the Mississippi
and down, down even farther
all the way down to New Orleans
so in the middle of those mosquito infested
nights in that land without identity
floated up to the transistor radio under my pillow
and thus to me, my ear, my dreams
the comforting sound of a reggae beat.
Others whom I've known who departed
physically from Indiana
to here or to the East
spent their time trying to wash
the Hoosier taste off their tongues.
I, on the other hand,
have clung to all of Indiana
I could tote here in a paper sack,
or carry in the pocket of my shirt,
or maintain always percolating
in my weak and overtaxed brain.
In fact, much of each of my days
I devote to the life I knew
or can imagine in the place,
that part of Indiana,
that part, and maybe all,
that ceased to exist
at least fifty years ago.
Still the roads and many of the woods
are recognizable on Google Earth.
The last time I was in my hometown,
I failed to spot another human being;
no dog even walked the streets.
Into a ghost town
almost any memory can come to life

even those that were once real enough
to etch deeply on a pane of sagging glass
itself transparent quattrocento drifts of snow
the story of love's disappointment
time's brevity and the hopeless possibility.
Life lurks there still of course
but its heartbeat and mine
no longer synchronous
I can only see in the rain falling
on the empty silo by the mill
a brachiosaurus with its tail laid out
along the now defunct railroad track.

TRILL

Paul E Anderson

The effect is like jotting down a note
to remember something later

A bird song
a series of notes

I have been engaged in an interior monologue
for most of my life

Poetry is stopping talking
listening

Trino

El efecto es como escribir una nota
Para recordar algo mas tarde

Canto de los pájaros
Una serie de notas

He estado involucrado en monólogos interiores
Durante la mayor parte de mi vida

La poesía se detiene y habla
Estoy escuchando

トリル

効果はメモを書き留めるようなものです
後で何かを覚えるために

鳥の歌

一連のメモ

私はインテリアモノローグに携わってきました
私の人生のほとんどのために

詩が止まって話している
聞いている

трель

Эффект похож на написание заметки
Вспомнить что-нибудь позже

Песня птиц
Серия заметок

Я был вовлечен во внутренние монологи
Большую часть моей жизни

Поэзия останавливается и говорит
Я слушаю

猫

Cat

猫は人間ではない。

A cat is not human.

猫は椅子の上で寝ている。

The cat is sleeping on the chair.

https://www.nihongomaster.com/dictionary/entry/44938/neko

Cat - Paul E Anderson

BOX

Colette Marsden

Dog bed	Dusty hairs	Sneezes	Spital	Choo
Sticky keys	Odd notes	**Shadow of hands**	Missing teeth	Whistles
Large rooms	Others in shades	Lacerated skin	Self absorption	Steam
Hunting	Lost in valleys	Eeriness	Creaking wings	Motion

HONEYCOMB

Paul E Anderson

Hooks	Feathers	Doll's eye	Photograph of a hand, folded	Rust
Cartoon	Tinfoil	Pennies	Thread	Swim
Skim	Hay	Shard	Half compact	Bolts
Flour	Washers	Springs	Dust	Ants

HOW CAN THE FUTURE BE A LIE?

Mike New

How can dirt truth a human invention
like lying and believing an end exists
that justifies any means
know?

My gloves aren't gloves only
when they become my gloves
instrumentally defining me to myself.

I am the bowsaw and the ax.
I am the grass that grows between the onions
and naturally the onions too, I am.

I am the plums that now I hear plopping on the ground
in the hot hollow of the dark still night
like striking a taut bass drum
the purple plum's skin explodes.

Truth,
part of the hocus pocus
producing the illusion of knowledge,
trod too with its own cross to Golgotha
where it with God died.

Being now without God and truth
lying becomes a meaningless concept
tossed out a car window
on the side of a country road
like Plato and Aquinas
with the chicken bone
beer bottle and an empty pack of Marlboros.

Since our best current scientific evidence
strongly suggests that everyone lies,
claiming to know when someone is lying

amounts to little more than
claiming that tomorrow
the sun will rise
even hotter than today.

We all know when someone is lying;
we just don't care.
We realize the person is merely
self-protectively creating a fiction
about himself or hers.

In fact, in this modern age,
thrust along by Machiavelli and Nietzsche,
everyone expects everyone else to lie.
Lying, like drinking alcohol
the two often find themselves together
lubricates the tensions of being in a roomful of people
you don't really like or trust
trying to pretend not only happiness and joy
but the requisite sincerity.
Feigning sincerity we often lie.

Even scientists lie,
fake data, claim results
unconfirmable by other scientists
in other laboratories.

With truth, like God, no more useful
in any sense other than archaeological,
since people have learned
that no reason exists not to go
on using the selfish instincts
from back when the world was as simple
as the bacterial world in a stagnant pond
where cattle drink urinate defecate
without a need to lie.

If you could have imagined it,
you would have seen the problem beforehand.
Enthrone fallibility as our new god.

Let us admit that everything's going to fail.
Survival requires we anticipate those failures
so that we can adjust circumstances
in time to avoid or mitigate them
making, with this legerdemain,
the future a lie.

SONG

Paul E Anderson

A half sonnet
should fit on a gro-
cery list, drawn on
the back of a gro-
cery receipt. Get
tuna fish, eggs, ba-
king soda, psyllium
(sp?
The reverse side is
intention. The printed
side realization. Too
much? Yes, but only
the cost, not the song
itself

Pelicans - Judith Kirkwood

WHAT A SMILE SAYS

Mike New

for Olivia Byard

>Why does the happy baby grin
>
>so soon a stranger in a hostile world?
>
>The night before a battle,
>
>Spartan warriors
>
>recited poetry,
>
>sang songs,
>
>danced,
>
>and performed farces
>
>preparing themselves to die

the next day.
At what moment does the system
nucleolus to phospholipid membrane
first become what we call "joyous"?
The secret signal from the soul
that says being in a mother's arm
being kept from falling by a father's hand
or being the arms
or being the hands
this we'll confess before
we've learned
to hide what we know
without words,
that we believe enough
if not much compared
to all the pain
if measured by the gain
in hope over hopelessness
by two infinitely magnified
like the joyous baby's smile
and the one who sees it.

Seal - Sarah Lyons

SLIPPING

Sybil Paradiso

Three score ten and I begin to see myself missing cues
Conceptual meaning has altered.
I no longer follow someone else's recipe...
I have found my own life's potion and it isn't for everybody.
The spells of my past reside with me like ravens
Unobtrusively waiting for their next assignment.

WIND IN THE TULIP TREE

Paul E Anderson

The wind in the Tulip Tree
Sea
Diminutive twitters
Trucks on 465
a motorcycle on Hanna Ave
A bell
The ebb and flow
Dogs barking
Children on a trampoline
Soundless clouds
Shadows on the ground
A honking car

Judith Kirkwood The observed life. Love it. I fact, I think I prefer Wind in the Tulip Tree to Wind in the Willows. I mean you could actually get whipped by wind in the willows - if you were under the willow. Now I miss the under the willow tree in our neighborhood in Madison where I used to take Jake as a child to play. My favorite years were raising young children. As long as I had enough adult getaways.
Colette Marsden Sounds heavenly
Sybil Paradiso Tulip tree?
Judith Kirkwood My mother in law had one in Springfield, IL
Sybil Paradiso Judith Kirkwood is it really a tree of tulips?

Before the Storm -Sybil Paradiso

CPSIA information can be obtained
at www.ICGtesting.com
Printed in the USA
BVHW021405100719
553077BV00003B/7/P